Walk Easy on the Earth

Walk Easy on the Earth

James Kavanaugh

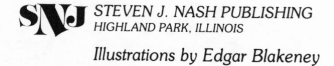

STEVEN J. NASH PUBLISHING
HIGHLAND PARK, ILLINOIS

Illustrations by Edgar Blakeney

OTHER BOOKS BY JAMES KAVANAUGH

NON-FICTION

There's Two Of You
Man In Search of God
Journal of Renewal
A Modern Priest Looks At His Outdated Church
The Struggle Of the Unbeliever (Limited Edition)
The Birth of God
Between Man and Woman (co-authored)
Search: A Guide For Those Who Dare Ask Of Life Everything Good and Beautiful

POETRY

There Are Men Too Gentle To Live Among Wolves
Will You Be My Friend?
Faces In The City
America: A Ballad
The Crooked Angel (children's book)
Sunshine Days and Foggy Nights
Maybe If I Loved You More
Winter Has Lasted Too Long
Walk Easy On the Earth
Laughing Down Lonely Canyons
Today I Wondered About Love (Adaptation of: Will You Still Love Me?)
From Loneliness To Love
Tears and Laughter Of A Man's Soul

FICTION:

A Coward For Them All
The Celibates

ALLEGORY:

Celebrate the Sun: A Love Story
A Village Called Harmony — A Fable

WALK EASY ON THE EARTH

First published by E.P. Dutton, New York (5 printings)   ISBN # 0-525-93078-7

Newly published in the U.S.A. by:
    Steven J. Nash Publishing   Library of Congress # 90-062056
    P.O. Box 2115
    Highland Park, IL 60035   ISBN # 1-878995-00-6

First Steven J. Nash Printing 1990   6th Printing Overall

6   7   8   9   10   11   12   13   14   15

To those who know:

       that the desert flowers will bloom
          when the oil rigs are silent;

       that trees will again stand tall
          over the ashes of forgotten wars;

       that no one can take away the sunrise
          or the smells of spring.

To those:
       who walk easy on the earth.

Introduction

Lately the world seems a more frightening place than before: fierce civil and territorial wars, a devouring inflation, and prophets speaking ominously of society's doom. It is as if our planet is finally out of fuel and will dissolve in its own anxiety.

Some people are turning to religion, others are amassing property or secretly hoarding gold. Almost everyone seems afraid of something. We live in sober, unlaughing, intensely serious days when men and women focus on personal survival and walk ponderously on the earth.

Such heaviness ignores the deeper human appetites to live creatively and joyously, appetites which have endured every historical crisis and flourished. To ignore them is to be obsessed with each new anxiety in the world's headlines. It is to focus on personal success and to hope that enough money or power will bring peace.

So much of life is decided by what we permit ourselves to see. If our focus is narrowly financial, we are terrified by the dismal vision of economists. If past failure is our obsession, we lose faith in private dreams. If guilt, we assume our own existence has no meaning and spend our lives vainly trying to please someone else. Only some recurring depression reveals a profound despair that resists any but the most dramatic redemption.

There is no need for redemption when I am in touch with the roots of my own human joy. I do not focus on a world's despair, I am forever renewed by spring splashing over granite rocks or a cautious deer emerging into twilight. I know then that I will survive all personal fears and economic disasters, that I will realize my finest dreams. At such times I am able to laugh easily, to see clearly, to reach out to another.

But when I lose contact with myself, I rely on someone else's approval or cautious wisdom, or the feeble security of success. I push and prod and force my way, upsetting the rhythm of my own energy, ignoring my secret strength and impossible resiliency. I become the ready victim of another's projected fears and private manipulations.

This is a book about refusing to surrender my life or dreams to anyone. It is not a guidebook or even a philosophy. It is the hand of a friend, the voice and face of one who lives in the same troubled, anxious world as you do, who shares the same guilt and fear. It is an attempt to respect my own deepest rhythms. It is an effort to rise above Asian wars and Arab oil, to look beyond inflation and even death, while staring them in the face, to laugh frequently amid occasional tears. It is, above all, to *Walk Easy on the Earth*.

JAMES KAVANAUGH
Nevada City, California

Walk Easy on the Earth

This Above All

Walk easy on the earth
  Without disturbing the sand.
Let others observe your footprints,
  But like night and day leave no trace.
Let your shadow move where it will,
  Its magnitude decided by the sun.

Do not love easily but well,
  Linked in spirit and flesh.
Let your love be warm and generous,
  And like the sun do not measure your gift.
Let your friendship be enduring and loyal,
  Even as the mountains are not displaced.

Let no one judge you
  Beyond what you actually do.
Thus you will not be judged
  By anyone harsher than yourself.
To judge another is to become blind
  And delay your own passage.

Do not disturb the waters
   Or race futilely against the wind.
The sun will rise every day
   And the moon will follow its course.
There is a rhythm for you
   As smooth and unmistaken as the tide.

Do not try relentlessly to understand.
   Time itself will decide.
There will be stars enough
   When clouds and neon lights do not hide them.
Do not be sad. It has been written for you:
   Your joy will come when it is time.

But this above all. Walk easy on the earth!

Seven Sons

Seven sons at a family meal
Who never knew they were young,
Only tomorrow and forever were real
And death would never come.
Football in fall and baseball in spring,
Where did time go so fast?
Where are the songs we promised to sing?
Where are the boys of the past?

We buried one a year ago spring,
Thirty years before it was time,
Another year came and another was gone
Before he could fall from the vine.
Each one I loved far more than I knew,
I think of them both every day
And the pain that I feel will never be healed,
There was so much I wanted to say.

Seven sons at a family meal
Who never knew they were young,
Only tomorrow and forever were real
And death would never come.
Football in fall and baseball in spring,
Where did time go so fast?
Where are the songs we promised to sing?
Where are the boys of the past?

Somewhere in My Heart

Somewhere in my heart
  A lonely shepherd laughs across Irish hills
  With no good reason even to smile,
  An indentured slave, forbidden suffrage or school,
  Denied land or grave, the helpless tool
  Of history's tyrants. Indebted for the clothes
  Upon his back, yet finally unafraid of those
  Who could not destroy his secret faith
  Or soothe the ancient anger of his race.
    Time was on his side,
    As was his Irish pride,
    That stubbornly refused to die
      And even laughed at funerals.

Somewhere in my heart
  A homespun girl laughs across Irish hills
  With no good reason even to smile,
  A shy domestic hating the clammy hand she fed,
  Denied her own hearth and a marriage bed
  By history's jailers. Kneeling on all fours
  To clean the foul-smelling floors
  Of those who mocked her brogue and auburn hair,
  But could not suppress the wrath of silent prayer.
    Time was on her side
    As was her Irish pride,
    That stubbornly refused to die
    And even laughed at funerals.

Somewhere in my heart.

Words Are My Friends

Words are my friends
    Sounds and syllables borrowed from sea shores
    And winds whispering across a lonely canyon,
    Or sudden storms frightening trees and little birds.
Words are my friends
    Born in silence and boyhood wanderings,
    Erupting from caves and rocks and city streets,
    Or seeping from wounds and a face wrinkled too soon.
Words are my friends
    Crawling from dreams and forgotten memories,
    Cursing at pain and the deaths I did not understand,
    Ready to hide or reveal as I bade them.

Words have carried my love
    Betrayed my enmity and fear,
    Healed wounds or inflicted them,
    Shared secrets or sheltered me from everyone.
Words are my friends.

I Asked the River

I asked the river
   Where he was going
      and how he would know
      when he got there.
He only laughed at me
   Splashing across the rocks.

I asked the mountain
   When he was high enough
      and how he would know
      when he reached the heavens.
His echo only laughed
   Like thunder in the valleys.

I asked the trees
   How long they would live
      and how they would know
      when they were a forest.
Their leaves only shook with mirth
   In the joy of a sudden wind storm.

Finally I was silent,
   As if there were no one else to please,
And I spent my time laughing
   With the river, the mountain,
      and trees.

It's Time to Fall in Love Again

It's time to fall in love again,
   The trout aren't biting in my favorite brook,
   I can't hear the lyrics of the willow trees,
   No one cares that the swallows didn't return,
   And the nest is empty under the eastern eaves.
   The wood ducks aren't playing by the upper pond,
   I can't see the moonlight through the sugar pine.
   (You know, the one I wanted bulbs on for Christmas,
   And you said a single star would do just fine.)

It's time to fall in love again,
   The lizards don't hide beneath the rocks,
   The waterfall has lost some silver in the sun,
   The brush is growing back across the forest path,
   I think the mockingbird has lost his tongue.
   The deer don't drink below the spring,
   Where I promised you the finest summer wine.
   (You know, the place I loved you in the afternoon,
   And you said the cold water would be just fine.)

It's time to fall in love again,
   (I promised you a ring to make you mine.)
It's time to fall in love again,
   (You said a daffodil would do just fine.)

It's time to fall in love again.

To See You

To see you grown suddenly, unmistakably older,
Like the gray, winter landscape frozen desolate, saddens me.
An oak tree in March, with only stubborn patches of mistletoe
Clinging to dark limbs like scattered ornaments of Christmas,
Reminds me of the green, familiar days I struggle to recall.
And when I hear you laugh, more softly now, I remember
The excitement and inflection of a happy child, when spring
Erupted in your eyes and birds sang everywhere to celebrate
May and Mary and the beauty of your unending life. I was a boy,
And together you and I walked among the magic of red tulips,
Standing like proud chalices, or the fragile purple iris
Waving like silk handkerchiefs in the soft hands of angels,
And we marveled at the fragrant peonies blushing pink
Like young nuns. Orange poppies like butterflies' wings
And most of all your roses, of every size and hue, that
Somehow reminded you of God and whispered to me of funerals.
Those were our very best days, your face most radiant,
My heart most free, and all of life a gentle, springtime mystery
We knew would never end, nor could we ever be as innocent again.
To see you grown suddenly, unmistakably older, saddens me,
But I know that somehow beyond all words and wounds, beyond
Time and pain and the mystery of death that makes me cry,
We will walk again amid the flowers of spring, just you and I.

When I Was a Boy

When I was a boy, it did not seem difficult to be a man.
After all, my father was a man, my mother a woman,
   And even at my age the differences were clearly pronounced.
Religion made the choice less obvious,
    Holy men wore skirts
    Holy women slept alone
And to be angry and lusting were not virtues well received.
When I left religion, for whatever reason, I tried psychology,
Probably because it was in vogue and took itself as seriously as religion.
Thus the transition was barely painful.
In therapy, however, I learned that men were more docile
    than I had remembered,
And women were far more aggressive and often swore like men.
When I left psychology, for whatever reason, I turned to social intercourse
    (probably an infelicitous word choice)
Only to discover that there was no solid line of demarcation
      between man and woman.
In fact, I met an increasing number of women who reminded me
    of the worst qualities of my father,
And countless men who reminded me of the distortions of my mother,
And I was frequently reminded that none of this mattered.
Thus homosexuality was as normal as blueberry pie,
And blueberry pie was as normal as I falsely thought
    my mother and father were.
Then it occurred to me that if there were the right man for the right man,
And the right women for the right woman, as was maintained,
There might even be the right woman, not unlike my mother,
For a man who was not unlike his father. This relieved me.
And even as when I was a boy,
    It did not seem difficult to be a man.

Donald

Donald lives with his mother
And everyone says that's ridiculous
For a forty-two-year-old man with a good job.
But Donald tried making it alone
Until it got too lonely in the morning.
Besides, his mother is nice and makes very good coffee.

Martin thinks Donald is a latent queer,
But Martin thinks that about almost everyone—
Which sometimes makes me wonder latently about Martin.

Mrs. Carmody says she'd never do what Donald's mother did,
But she doesn't say what Donald's mother did.
Not admit her only son hasn't spoken to her in ten years.

Betty Lou is certain that Donald is impotent,
Which probably explains why Betty Lou's husband works nights.

Dr. Adcock suggested over martinis that it was an oral fixation
Aptly symbolized by Donald's hysterical overbite.
Adcock did not reveal the symbolism of his own elongated incisors.

Madge Lewis thinks Donald is afraid of women,
And he is, of Madge Lewis. But then so is everyone else.

Eddie Lewis says Donald is the kind you read about
That chokes his mother and buries her in the backyard.
Which is exactly what Eddie Lewis would like to do with Madge.

Donald says that when he lived alone
   It got too lonely in the morning.
Besides, his mother is nice,
   And makes very good coffee.

"Walk easy on the earth
  Without disturbing the sand.
Let others observe your footprints,
  But like night and day leave no trace.
Let your shadow move where it will,
  Its magnitude decided by the sun . . ."

You Are Not My Fantasy

You are not my fantasy
   Of sheer rock cliffs crowned by redwoods,
   No silver waterfall cascading into white rapids,
   Not a damp green meadow cooled by cypress trees.
You are only a landscape I've learned to love,
   A scrub oak plain and beautiful,
   An awkward jack pine more comforting than any willow,
   Dry brown grass grown golden in the twilight,
   A granite rock hiding under dark moss,
   A mysterious madrone with sculpted copper limbs,
   A friendly gulch mined to bedrock and fresh water.
I've seen enough white mountain cliffs and waterfalls,
   Enough green meadows and azure lakes
      That are more beautiful in the distance.
I want the familiar landscape that I've grown to love,
   The scrub oaks and golden grass,
   The red madrone and granite hidden under green moss,
   Fresh water and the promise of twilight.

Jed

Jed's a well-digger in the mountains.
　　("The freedom agrees with me.")
I doubt I've known a happier man.
　　("Why the hell shouldn't I be?")

He coulda been rich if he wanted.
　　("It just gets in the way.")
He never charged what he shoulda.
　　("Some of 'em just can't pay.")

He made just enough to care for his folks.
　　("They're going on ninety-three.")
And a daughter with four whose man died broke.
　　("He got in the way of a tree.")

A retarded son who worked on the wells.
　　("As kind as a kid every was.")
A couple of gypsies who happened along.
　　("They really had no one but us.")

Jed never paid tax, he voted just once.
　　("Didn't change things a bit.")
He never asked for a cent from the bank.
　　("Them fellers ain't worth a shit.")

A year ago spring his wife passed away.
　　("She lived as long as she could.")
He built her a coffin and prayed at her grave.
　　("I never knew no one as good.")

The night before last Jed joined her at rest.
　　("The freedom agrees with me.")
I doubt I have known a happier man.
　　("Why the hell shouldn't I be?")

Reflections

It was hard to take
　　When the doctor who made me quit smoking
　　　　Got emphysema,
And the lawyer who handled my divorce case
　　Started wearing my old ties.
And when the priest who excommunicated me
　　Ran off with the Avon lady.
But you really start to worry
　　When your accountant
　　　　Has an office at the racetrack!

Larry

Larry spent fourteen years
   trying to please his mother,
And nine years struggling
   to please his father.
He spent four years
   rushing to please his boss,
Ten years wanting to please his wife,
And twenty-six years
   determined to please his kids.
I thought the preacher
   summed it up well.
He said that Larry
   lived a pleasing life.

Life

Life is still
   a high school football game.
Every month
   someone new makes the team.
This one at fourteen,
   another at forty.

On Learning of
a Young Friend's Suicide

Society's scar, child dressed in man's clothes,
Too frightened to grow in quiet repose,
Condemned by time to be another one of those
   Without the tools to live.

Child of success and suburbs, too much too soon.
No need to struggle or to understand the moon.
Whatever happened to a bouncing red balloon
   And the belching laugh of boyhood?

Child shielded from dreams and discipline's wages,
Unattuned to postponed joys and the deeper rages
That distill energies and turn the pages
   Of life's surprises one by one.

Child old at birth, wrinkled by fate,
Forced to climb fences and ignore the gate
Until the path was gone and love too late
   To tell you that we cared.

Child loved as much as you could allow,
We tried helplessly to tell you how
When you could only understand the now
   Of recurring disappointments.

Perhaps a father's death was more than you could bear,
His absence the final emptiness in the air
That told you no one else could really care,
   Or smile so proudly.
   Or smile so proudly.

A Day in Court

The unsmiling judge with wet, flapping jowls,
Dismissing the tears of husbands and wives,
Spitting out consonants, rolling his vowels,
Tearing out hearts and carving up lives,
Slicing the children apart at their bowels,
Believing that justice latterly thrives—
Wiser than Solomon or blinking old owls—
As long as his echoing edict survives.

The unsmiling judge with stern eyes of stone,
Convinced that his honor will salvage our race,
Rages at crime from his emperor's throne,
With history's arrogance etched on his face,
Applauding his parents and disciplined home
Where all of the offspring emerged full of grace:
"For that which is reaped is only what's sown,"
Then he nods to his clerk to begin the next case.

The unsmiling judge can relax a bit now
While lawyers bow humbly like prep school boys,
A touch of a grin unfurls his brow,
Capriciously gone at the hint of a noise.
He lowers his gavel and narrows his eyes,
No Shah or Napoleon sat more entrenched,
Political puppet whose whims govern lives,
Who paid enough ransom to sit on the bench.

The unsmiling judge who decides in our stead
That petulance lives and justice is dead.
I'd rather be judged by the least of our race,
Than the unsmiling judge with the arrogant face.

Enough Sanity

I've had enough sanity.
The trees and I will go crazy again,
   Unproductive and lazy again,
   Whispering secrets no one dares to share.
Who has advice that does not mask fear?
Who has wisdom that takes time to hear?
   Lawyers need lawyers,
   Doctors lust to die,
   Bankers sweat for money,
   No one wonders why.
Masters have masters, only fools are free,
Presently I've had enough of all your sanity.
   The trees and I will go crazy again,
   Unproductive and lazy again,
Whispering secrets no one dares to share.

Yesterday Afternoon

Yesterday afternoon I decided, decisively,
  To build an orphanage on fifteen acres.
In the evening I planned my own commune
  Which would include plumbing and clean napkins.
This morning I knew I had to get married and have seven kids
  —Like my father—
An hour ago I determined to build a house
  And raise potatoes and summer squash with my own hands.
I wonder if that buxom girl in the granny dress
  Would love me if she got to know me,
  And help build the house.
I wish to hell I'd get my laundry done and fix the kitchen sink.

Old Jesse

I wonder whatever happened to old Jesse,
Galloping around the schoolyard on his imaginary horse
    at ten or twelve
When the rest of us gave up our fantasies at seven
And spent our recess trying to knock a softball
    over an old stone wall by a railroad track.
How we laughed at old Jesse, slapping his ass
    with that imaginary whip,
Turning a dusty playground into an endless prairie,
And chasing his dreams across the hills to free flowing rivers.
All those years I never asked him about the Indians in the trees,
The cattle snorting their way to death in Texas,
The whistle of a train announcing the end of covered wagons
    and the birth of real progress.
I grew big enough to hit that softball over the fence, but never far enough,
And the others managed college or a job, and the family everyone expected.
But I wonder whatever happened to old Jesse,
If he finally settled down like the rest, to kids
    and hitting a softball and going home for dinner.
God, I hope he's still out there somewhere, galloping on that same old horse,
Feeling the dust in his nostrils and the sweat rolling down his cheek,
Watching the sun slip behind a mountain and hearing
    the coyotes sing to his campfire,
Still eager for another morning when he'll roam that endless prairie
And chase his dreams across the hills to free flowing rivers.

I Brood Too Much

I brood too much.
You're right: It never leads anywhere.
  Nor will it.
I brood too much:
  So many hopes gone awry,
  So many reasons to cry,
  Too long alone with the sky,
  Wondering why,
    Wondering why.
I brood too much.
You're right: It never leads anywhere.
Which is something else to brood about.

The Accountant

My father used to have a bookkeeper,
A wry, tattered man with thick glasses and shiny pants,
Who lisped a little, spoke softly,
   And called my father "Sir."
We felt sorry for him and gave him a turkey for Christmas.
Mother made scarves and sugar cookies for his children
   And gave her old brown coat to his wife.
I liked him because he gave me a gum eraser and two pencils.
No one seems to remember his name.
I think it was Al.
   Or was it Art?

I have an accountant,
A crisp, tailored man with Hollywood glasses and a pinky diamond,
Who scowls at my crumpled receipts and missing records.
He calls me "guy" and I apologize for his inconvenience.
His hand moves on the calculator like a surgeon's.
I tap my pencil, wish the phone would ring,
And make more coffee. He requests Sanka.
At Christmas he sends me a bottle of Cutty Sark.
His name is Fitzen, Hamel, Schuster, Agaganian, and O'Meara.
   His bill is almost as long.

I wish to hell I could remember that bookkeeper's name.

Well, the Bank Turned Me Down

Well, the bank turned me down on my loan
  And it's probably my own fault
  Because I keep searching for the old-time banker,
    A look-you-in-the-eye, seat-of-the-pants guy
  Who didn't trust credit checks and hardly asked a question
    If he knew your father.
I was insulted by the fidgety replacement, a computer-fingered boy
  Who stripped me to my financial shorts and demanded
  Ten times the assets needed to repay a small loan
    Backed by my land, house, and car,
  Not to mention, furniture, my stereo, and an old Winchester.
It was hard not to spit on the floor but I kept waiting to be rescued
  By the warm, fatherly banker of the TV ads who only wants
    To help the poor buy homes and to assist
    Short, fat men to own their own businesses.
But there was only this pimply high school boy drumming his fingers
  And asking a lot of things that were none of his concern,
    Like, "Why do you really want the money?"
    ("To spend, you asshole!")
That's probably when it happened. I moved closer to his desk,
  And a voice that sounded like mine whispered,
    "You're not gonna believe this, but there's these three ships,
    "The *Nina,* the *Pinta,* and the *Santa Maria,*
  "And we got it on good authority, if we go due west . . ."

"I am heroless save for the peasants in rice paddies
And the wrinkled grandmother squinting rapturously
her smile into the sun,
With a baby's brown face pressed against
her complexion of a fragrant, decaying apple..."

I Am But a Part of It All

I am but a part of it all,
No more or less important
Than the cab driver in Manila
Who weeps with joy over the grandchild
   That makes his life newly worthwhile
With such radiance I have rarely known,
Such pure joy that usually eludes me
   With my options and optical illusions.
He is a beautiful man, still naive enough
To love MacArthur and name an eldest son Arturo,
Still grateful enough to remember Bataan
   Beyond any politics or government compromise,
Trusting enough to love God and have heroes.
I am heroless save for the peasants in rice paddies
   And the wrinkled grandmother squinting rapturously
      her smile into the sun,
   With a baby's brown face pressed against
      her complexion of a fragrant, decaying apple.
Heroless save for anyone who can still laugh easily
   Or stare silently in awe at a disappearing sun.
I am a man bursting with a strange love
   That finds ought but a child's memories to worship.
My own land has become an exploding real estate market,
   My own friends with no time to pluck blades of grass
      And whistle their wonder for the day,
Seeking instead victories that time has proved a thousand times
   Are not victorious,
Seeking them with such passion and enthusiasm
   That I am ashamed to tell them about a cab driver in Manila
And that I am but a part of it all.

Walking Through a Market in a Philippine Village

Why are they smiling so?
Have they not heard the distant drums
   That beat of greed and revolution?
Don't they know that love grows tired
     And children grow up to move away?
Don't they know that yesterday is silent
     And tomorrow is only one more day?

Why are they smiling so?
Have they not heard the distant bells
     That ring of pain and disappointment?
Don't they know that time is unforgiving
     And lovers grow silent when they leave?
Don't they know that dreams are dying
     And only madmen dare to be free?

Why are they smiling so?
     Condemned to poverty from birth.
Why are they smiling so?
     As if the meek still inherit the earth.

Why are they smiling so?

The Peasant Survives

The peasant survives
   Despite three degrees
      and two tailor-made suits,
   A taste for French wine
      and hand-stitched cowboy boots.
He still prefers
   Mashed potatoes and pork gravy
      to any souffle you can name,
   Duck hunting to a symphony
      and few things to a football game.
He doesn't sip, he drinks,
   He doesn't taste, he devours.
He talks before he thinks,
   He doesn't bathe, he showers.
Ulysses and *Gatsby* put him to sleep,
   He is the most uncultured of men.
Years of Jesuit logic won't guarantee
   He'll ever behave rationally again.

Beyond a Misty Hill

Some people never go there,
   Perhaps they never will.
There's an unmarked road
To a silent grove
   Beyond a misty hill.
They don't send invitations,
   I doubt they ever will.
You walk alone
To a place I've known
   Beyond a misty hill.
Most will never find it,
   For life's daily drill,
But the ones like me
Find a kind of peace
   Beyond a misty hill.
There are no maps describing,
   It can't be found by skill.
It's an unmarked road
To a silent grove
   Beyond a misty hill.
It's an unmarked road to a silent grove
   Beyond a misty hill.

"You walk alone
To a place I've known
  Beyond a misty hill . . ."

Lately, Most of My Friends

Lately, most of my friends are into making money,
And with the rising toll of inflation, they are convinced
    That the only suitable protection
      Is more money.
Our conversation, which used to cover good vacation spots
    or a recent play,
Now focuses on land in South America or corn in May.
Even our reading of politics or current fiction
Has lately been replaced by the same addiction
    Of when to sell or when to wait,
    Or the cheapest way to incorporate.
Eddie sees the future in diamonds,
    Brock still leans toward gold,
Frank believes in property
    And tax-free bonds, I'm told.
Even Jeanie is remodeling,
    Making a hundred grand a year.
Sally has converted to computers,
    Trying to program out her fear.

They all think I'm crazy
For passing up each new deal.
What they don't know won't hurt 'em:
    I'm learning to steal!

I Forgot How Beautiful It Was

I forgot how beautiful it was, the spring, I mean,
With daffodils strewn like careless gold nuggets
Across the ravine and purple streams of iris flowing
Suddenly overnight, a trout leaping for a May fly
At the edge of a sunlit riffle to celebrate an escape
From winter and the lonely depths of a dark reservoir
    Not unlike mine.

I forgot how beautiful it was, the spring, I mean,
Amid a friend's death in December and ever new fears
Manufactured and classified jealously from everywhere
By newsmakers and baritone rumor mongers of a sad world.
Tonight, when they groaned of gas shortages and suicides,
Decomposed bodies in Chicago and a dog bite in Dallas,
    I lost myself in soft rain.

I forgot how beautiful is was, the spring, I mean,
And I didn't care what Texaco stole or who died in Iran,
What the dollar brought in Tokyo or land in California.
I was only grateful for green hills and a belching bullfrog,
Two deer trembling on a gravel road and a salamander
Slithering home for dinner, and wondered why I forgot
    How beautiful it was.

Eddie and Denise

Eddie and Denise were a perfect match, she with her shy smile,
    and he with his broad shoulders and 3.9 average.
They got married and constructed a cautious economy, including
    house, car, furniture, microwave, cassette TV,
        and 4% for entertainment.
He worked unsparingly, she made her own clothes, and
    at the end of four years they owed $61,000
And had $124 in a joint savings account.

Edward and Dennison moved with three teenagers to Vernal Acres
    when he became the firm's youngest vice-president.
With two in college and a guitar-shaped pool, they still managed
    the tennis club, Hawaii, and a mountain cabin.
They invested in a Baja motel, an apple fritter franchise in Texas,
    and studied the future of soybeans.

EJ and Denny celebrated forty-two years of marriage just before EJ retired.
The wooded mansion was almost paid for, the stock market was up,
    Texas loved apple fritters, and real estate values had made them wealthy.
When they left for a trip to China, the broker advised
    that soybeans looked strong.

Three months later they returned prematurely when EJ's back flared,
    Denny bowed to dysentery, and the accountant was concerned.
The Baja motel had slipped into the Pacific, soybeans had died,
    and the apple fritter franchise had been caught using preservatives.
With 15% inflation EJ sold the cabin, mortgaged the house,
    and went back to work.
At the end of forty-four years together, they owned $61,000
    and had $124 in a joint savings account.

Grimy Rivers

Grimy rivers make me sad,
    Mocking the melting snow and bubbling springs
      that filled them with sparkling life,
    Denying the history that made rivers
      the highways to each new civilization
    Scorning the children and dreamers
      who wander with them to private worlds,
    Despising the lonely and homeless
      who are healed by the river's music.
I do not think I have ever been so sad
    That clear waters rushing over rocks
      could not calm my soul,
    Or the dark, clean drift of a wise river
      could not free me from some inherited pain.
Even if all were gone,
    I would lie motionless in shallow river waters
      and let them wash me like the rocks
    To some new life
    Pure and beautiful
    Beyond time.
Where there are no grimy rivers to make me sad.

It Makes You Wonder

It makes you wonder
    When a decent, god-fearing man buys a new building
    He doesn't need or want, and actually doesn't even like,
    To shelter income with double depreciation
      (even though the building is wildly appreciating).
    And despite the substantially negative cash flow which ensues,
    He makes a profit he doesn't really deserve and which benefits
    No one except the god-fearing man and the bank that staked him.
Like I say, it makes you wonder,
    What the hell you tell a little kid
    When he asks you if it's wrong to steal.

If There Is a Hell

If there is a hell, it surely must be
    All the game show hosts locked in a single room forever,
    Laughing and shouting at each other,
    With a new game following every old one
    And an old one after every new one,
    And so on *ad infinitum* as befits any decent hell,
    Each one shouting louder and laughing more outrageously,
    Proclaiming more surely and promising more lavishly
    Until hell becomes heaven and heaven hell,
    And all the luggage and cars and new kitchens,
    The dream vacations and major appliances reach the ceiling,
    Then the TVs and stereos, tape decks and cassettes
    Boom in unison with all the laughs and shouts
    Until the whole room breaks its lungs and splits its sides.
    Finally there is only silence and a quiet voice announces:
    "This has all been a game!"
Then the madness begins again.

Ambitious Dan

Ambitious Dan was an active man
    Who strove for strength and power.
He worked at his desk with unflagging zest,
    Each minute of every hour.

He married a wife at a quarter past five,
    And was back to work at six.
His kids were born at the crack of dawn,
    Ten minutes from his desk.

When his time had come and life was done,
    He couldn't find time to die.
So they moved his desk at his dying breath
    To an office in the sky.

There are times at night when the sky is bright,
    You can catch a glimpse of Dan,
Just a trifle west he's at his desk,
    A damned successful man!

The Theorists

Androgyny and love seminars
   And worn old men and women of every age
      Turning their memories and regrets into theories,
      Deciding what is love and sex and eternity
         For anyone who will listen,
      Promising understanding to the old
         And resignation to the middle-aged,
      Giving death a new name and new currency
         To graying hair and wrinkled groins.
The theories are well meaning,
   Providing the theorists another reason to stay alive.
I have no such understanding,
   Grateful that the sun will not be gone until I die.

Did I Tell You?

Did I tell you that my father died, a warm, powerful man,
Laughing and boisterous, brooding and awkward and far too proud,
Who loved me so helplessly that he beamed whenever he saw me?
Even now I wait for that reassuring smile around a corner,
Wait for him to muss my hair and throw me in the air and tell me
That no boy could ever bring half as much joy to his father.
In the haze of his death, even his flaws seem vastly irrelevant
And it only hurts to realize that a child sometimes misunderstood,
That an adolescent was embarrassed at what I now miss the most,
That even a young man was slow to comprehend and love him.
Now both are gone in time's impatience and disregard of feeling,
So I am left to wonder if father or his son will ever return.
Day follows day and when I fear that I will at last become
As plain and unremarkable as my father swore I'd never be,
I search in vain for a too proud, irreplaceable smile to reassure me.

Looking for Yesterday

I am a soldier without a war,
   A sculptor without a stone,
I am a lion without a roar,
   A child without a home.
The skies are as silent as the streets,
   Nights as speechless as the days.
Tomorrow I'll take another plane
   And maybe find a place to stay.

Looking for yesterday in Shanghai,
   Walking nowhere today in Rangoon.
Searching the dark eyes of Bangkok,
   Studying an Indonesian moon.

I am a wind without a sail,
   A port without a storm,
I am a horse without a trail,
   A revolution yet unborn.
The skies are as silent as the streets,
   Nights as speechless as the days.
Tomorrow I'll take another plane
   And maybe find a place to stay.

Looking for yesterday in Shanghai,
   Walking nowhere today in Rangoon.
Searching the dark eyes of Bangkok,
   Studying an Indonesian moon.

There's No One to Be Lonely With

There's no one to be lonely with,
   No one who can barely smile,
Only chattering conversations,
   When will tears be in style?
I am weary of all the gladness,
   The grinning voices of the land,
Tonight I'll wallow in sadness
   And the tragic mystery of man.
How can I speak of yesterday
   When I don't know what to say?
How can I talk of tomorrow
   When words get in my way?
There's a language I never learned,
   A sadness I cannot reveal.
There's a courage that has deserted me,
   I cannot tell what I feel.
A tree is easy to chat with,
   The sky will say what it can.
Even the moon is responsive,
   The silence is only in man.
Find a tree that you love,
   Tell all your dreams to the sky,
Give up your lust to the moon,
   And please be as lonely as I.

Enough

Enough serenity and playing in the sun,
Enough pleasure and working to have fun.
Enough worry and the pursuit of things,
Enough leisure and the boredom it brings.
Enough success
   With the theft of every hour,
Enough investments
   With their artificial power.
Enough friends to organize my days,
Enough critics to analyze my ways.
Enough loneliness
Enough pain
Enough emptiness
Time to start again.

Of All Man's Gifts

Of all man's gifts
I admire passion most of all,
Passion for anything,
    Good or evil,
    Flesh or spirit.
I do not mean ambition or greed,
    Commitment and creed,
These are man-made substitutes, passionless.
I mean a passion that forgets self
    And ignores time,
    Transforming, expanding, renewing,
        Unafraid of undoing whatever has been done.
Passion has no master or teacher,
    All of life is its servant,
    It is curious about the whole world.
It lusts for sun and moon, is a friend of stars,
    Delights in storms and snow and the desert's heat.
No money can buy it,
    It is no respecter of sex or station,
        Race or education.
Without it eyes are dim and hearts faltering,
Without it death cannot come too soon.
    It has already arrived
    Only waiting to be announced.

Guilt

Guilt rides on his horse
   Like a weary soldier,
   Sharpening his sword
     and looking for a war,
Ready to make anyone's cause his own.
Then, when there is no war
   And no one needs him anymore,
   He wanders in circles
     wondering who he is.
Finally he dismounts
   And puts his sword away,
Feeling bad again
   Because he forgot to thank his horse.

"A brave, disciplined bird, content to fly together or alone . . ."

The Mallard

The hunter waits an alien in the chill morning's steel blue sunrise,
Knee-deep in shivering water, camouflaged against the icy skies
To lure the cautious mallard circling nervous decoys
And suspicious of each awkward color or discordant noise
   That threatens his survival.
A brave, disciplined bird, content to fly together or alone,
Too restless and independent to surrender to a final home,
Ready to drown in marsh grass suicide rather than die
A coward unable to shout his lonely freedom cry
   Across the heavens.
Now man and bird are locked in some ancient lovers' dance
Of hunter and the hunted, and man has but a fleeting chance
To still the beating wings and fierce, protesting flesh,
Then to savor gently each wild morsel of that hero's breast
   That died so badly.
Some will weep at the slaughter, curse the hunter and his gun
That sacrificed the soaring life of such a proud and fearless one.
I am content to toast his noble life, salute his warrior's art,
And promise to preserve intact the free, unfettered heart
   That flew so proudly.

It Is Destined

It is destined by some rhythm more powerful than religion or even
economics
That the earth belongs to us all or none shall possess it.
What Christianity never achieved nor Buddha, what Communism
    never won nor Muhammed,
Will finally ensue without prayer or sacred proclamation.
There is no good or bad, malice or virtue, only time and circumstance,
And the inexorable hand of a mysterious rhythm dictating
That art and love and understanding will flower
Or dust will inherit the earth.
What nobility could never teach, survival's law will demand.
The exploiter will be pitied when exploitation disappears.
What man refused to share will finally be taken away.
Even as I write in the Manila Hotel where MacArthur governed
And returned to Corregidor to drive out the Japanese,
His very grave is silent, but the Kamikazes return
    to go in business with the Filipinos.
Today America salutes Peking and Taiwan curses her treachery,
But tomorrow China will host Hong Kong in mutual celebration.
Not because of virtue or even political compromise,

But because man is destined to live lovingly on the earth.
Or he shall not live at all!
Not because of Mao or Marx, Jefferson or Jesus,
But because a rhythm as obvious as water and land
    governs the destiny of man.
Lion will lie with lamb or both be devoured by Leviathan.
Men will not turn swords to plowshares, but swords will rust,
Not because man is noble, but because it is written in reality.
Churches never really changed anyone, nor did a poem.
Asia is no wiser than the west, man no wiser than woman,
Black or brown virture no more enduring than yellow or white.
What socialism could not achieve or Iron Curtains,
    what democracies could not do nor kings and queens,
Will happen of itself!
The Arabs will not be proud because the earth gave them oil,
Nor America because its soil is lavish of wheat and corn.
All will be as one whether they will or no, and death will
    follow life like winter to spring and summer.
Thus it is written by man's own hand!

The Mourners

The mourners
   gather solemnly
      to weep at his funeral
   before it is time.
In the process
   they kill him.

Asia's New Aristocracy

Asia's new aristocracy rises from the ashes of Nagasaki,
   phoenix-like and not remembering Pearl Harbor at all,
Sacrificing Shinto to Sony and transforming the Emperor into a
   late-model Toyota,
Traversing the globe to storm duty-free shops for more Chanel No. 5
   and Chivas Regal,
A superrace at least as ugly as any American ever was,
Pleading for Aryan eyes, a Nordic nose, and a bust big enough
   to startle Confucius,
As inflated as the currency that turns yen into Zen, and provides
   the credentials history denied.
Thus Singapore's obelisk of Japanese atrocities is ignored,
   not in forgiveness but in deference to business,
And girls in Bangkok wait like hors d'ouevres under glass to endure
   the swords of a new Samurai selling computers.
Even Manila's cab drivers, old enough to remember intramural horror,
Smile benignly at Hitachis and sacrifice adolescents whose forebears
   gave their tongues and testicles to Hirohito.
But what the hell, let bygones be bygones, progress is vengeance enough,
What Bataan and Hiroshima could never do, affluence will accomplish
   without nuclear help.
Even now the Japanese businessmen die of heart attacks, Tokyo
   chokes on smog, flunking students commit a gentle hara-kiri,
And the once docile women, slowly liberated after centuries, scurry
   to their tennis lessons and drag their kids to orthodontists.
Actually, it occurs to me that if the Japanese
   Could only double government spending,
   Promise all of their citizens damn near everything,
   Antagonize the oil-producing nations,
   And pledge themselves to fight Communism anywhere in the world
They could become the greatest nation on earth and finally
   lose World War II.

There's Hardly a Place

There's hardly a place for madness anymore,
Docility the proper profile and faceless boredom.
How come all my neighbors look alike?
Clean-shaven and self-controlled.
No eruptions or savage screams for life,
Only enameled silence where everyone hides forever.
A man could live his whole life and know no one.
Are we the only crazies left on the earth?
Come, let us be mad together,
   Decadent, drooling fools,
   Unaffected by schools,
   Totally contemptuous of rules.
Come, let us be mad together,
   Laughing and sad,
   Raging and glad,
   Quite properly mad.
Or we will never love.

Classical Guitar in a Filipino Village

Untrained fingers moving like gentle waves
   across all the rills of my feelings,
Playing the sounds and songs
   learned on silent nights without electricity
   in a world that does not destroy my senses
     with the numbing disco of traffic and too many words.
Yours are a mother's hands
   that soothe her child to serenity and sleep,
A lover's lips that whisper with soft eloquence
   what passion could never say,
A god's fingers that created man
   from slime and confusion to this wonder.
I could listen to you for hours
   and lose my identity in your strumming.
You would trade it all for Levis
   and a rock band in Akron, Ohio.

Standing

Standing
  On the rim
    of the world
Holding back
  Lest I fall in.
Seems like
  I've been here
    A hundred years
Telling myself
  Tomorrow I'll begin.

Darlene

Well, Darlene came to my house for dinner and said
   She doesn't like men much anymore
   Because they all make money and ignore their kids,
   And only want sex, if they can get it up, which ain't often,
   But too damn often as far as she's concerned.

Well, Darlene finished her chicken Kiev and said
   That men turn women into wretched slaves
   And never let their wives do anything except have kids,
   Wash clothes, drive car pools to the Little League,
   Shop for food, then rush home in time to fix dinner.

Well, Darlene asked for more coffee and said
   She certainly hopes that ERA
   Will turn things around and bring men down,
   And give women a chance to run businesses and countries
   And all the things that men have made such a mess of.

Well, Darlene watched me clear the table and said
   I was full of it when I suggested that women
   Made fools of men with sexual power and little girl games,
   And bored men silly talking about nothing except trivia,
   Then took the kids and most everything else with the divorce.

Well, Darlene turned up my stereo and said she'd be glad
   When men no longer made servants of their wives.
I turned the stereo down and said I'd be just as glad
   when women don't leave men scarred and silent all their lives.
Then Darlene went home. I did the dishes. We did not have sex.

A Woman

You know it's hard for a boy when he tries to be human,
  To grow to a man and find a real woman.
I was just a little short for the basketball team,
I dribbled too slow, my passing was wild,
I couldn't get a date with the homecoming queen
  'Cause I danced like a drunk on a lumber pile.
  Just a shy little guy and I never knew why,
  I hadn't even lived when I wanted to die,
    Because I feared
    When I neared
  A sweet-smelling lady or a pretty-faced gal.
  I was everybody's buddy, the universal pal.
Well, the days went by and the years disappeared,
My freckles went away and my skin was clear,
But the ladies I got were the ones that were left,
And the ones that I wanted I couldn't get,
  Till I met
  Not a kitten in a basket or a prison made of lace,
  Not a lonely man's surrender or another pretty face.
  I met a woman.
I mean a woman!
  Old enough to see
  Young enough to believe
  Loved enough to love!

You know it's hard for a boy when he tries to be human
     To grow to be a man and to find his own woman.
It never really mattered that I ran like a rabbit,
That I talked to the birds, sang a song to the trees,
Sailed a kite over hills like a hawk in the breeze,
   When I tried to kiss a girl I always had to sneeze.
   Just a shy little guy and I never knew why,
   I hadn't even lived when I wanted to die,
     Because I feared
     When I neared
   A sweet-smelling lady or a pretty-faced gal.
   I was everybody's buddy, the universal pal.
Well, the time went by and my friends were gone,
And the days somehow didn't last as long.
The ladies I loved were the ones that were left
'Cause the ones that I wanted I couldn't get,
   Till I met
   Not a kitten in a basket or a prison made of lace,
   Not a lonely man's surrender or another pretty face.
   I met a woman.
I mean a woman!
     Scarred enough to see,
     Soft enough believe,
     Loved enough to love!
Loved enough to love!

Love Is As Much an Accident As Life

Love is as much an accident as life,
As much a mystery as death and pain,
  As capricious and uncertain
As the whims of a summer rain.
Love is what is at hand,
A city where I happened to be born,
  A tree or an acre of land,
A friendly bed that kept me warm.
A hand that eased my hurt, a breast,
  A place to drop my pack and rest.
Familiarity grown comfortable and more familiar.
  Love is life's refusal to be alone,
  Better an angry, silent home
    than all the darkness.
Love is whatever I want it to be,
  Love is whatever it seems to me.
So many words explaining it,
  So many songs proclaiming it.
Only a rare and precious love is free.

You Loved Me in Manila

You loved me in Manila
And called me Paul Newman
   Whom you had seen the night before on TV.
It flattered me profoundly that you saw the resemblance,
   That is until you showed me a picture of Brando
   Who had loved you the week before.
I still wasn't convinced
   Until Robert Redford grinned at you from a tour bus.

Thailand

Laughing land of poverty and magic,
    Where simple joys
        Have not yet disappeared.
Hong Kong calls and beguiling Tokyo,
    With electronic wealth
        And affluence to be cheered.
The price of rice will rise,
    Silk and cotton lose to new synthetics.
Then Buddha will close his eyes,
    And a westerner will teach them dianetics.

Of Culture and Sex and Alien Gods

In Bangkok, beautiful hostesses, with Buddha grinning
   from their cleavage,
Will sleep with anyone who says "I love you"
   with some show of sincerity
And is able to pay twenty-five dollars plus inflation.

In Manila, thanks to Christ, Magellan, and the colonials,
   it's only twenty bucks.
They undress more modestly, perform less sinfully
   without mentioning love,
While Jesus dies on a gold chain between two overcast breasts.

In America, any decent college graduate will undress before you've met,
   and roll a joint from her own stock.
Then she'll drive you home in the morning after breakfast,
   without charge or obligation.
Obviously I'm against prostitution.

Enough of Love for Now

Enough of love for now,
   Too many mouths to spare another forkful.
I am the lonely child of spontaneity and passing love
   that starves those born of parents.
I want no root in another's emptiness,
No love which makes me a headstone for my grave
   Or the unprotesting slave of life's illusions.
There is no time for love till I've seen the hills,
There may not be time at all, only enough hours
   To silence ancient voices
   And the slowly disappearing noises
      of some unhappy life.
I need no earthquake or tornado warning,
Only the night and a gentle morning,
   A place to write and rest, enough to eat,
   And a gentle breeze brushing my face
Against the wishes of the summer's heat.
Enough of love for now.

What of the Rootless Ones?

What of the rootless ones
   Who fail to find a place on the earth,
   Who have lost interest in Disneyland,
   And don't care if the Yankees win or lose
      Or if the Jews and Arabs make peace.
Each day is a new dream too ambitious,
Each hour a new hope too capricious
   Ever to be understood.
Time is running out except for the children,
   Who know life will last forever,
   Or the fearful ones who have already died.
Life has its limits too confining,
Hope has its boundaries too defining,
   And what of the rootless ones
Who fail to find a place on the earth?

Some Few Walk Easy

There are some few who walk easy on the earth,
Passing from childhood to wisdom without a usual turbulence,
Too aware to be young
Too alive ever to be old,
Contemporary and companion of every life
Beyond discrimination
Or explanation,
God's gift to His world
To make the lonely laugh
The neglected come alive
To stir spirits and warm hearts
To enrich the discordant parts
Of all the rest of life.
Such gentle ones make a lasting mark on every life they touch
Without trying or preaching, judging or seeking,
Merely by their presence on the earth.
A shade tree by a favorite stream
The morning sun on a damp meadow
A green hill mirrored in a quiet lake
A sugar pine silver in the moonlight
Until the morning comes and they are gone too soon,
Leaving us in darkness and unspeakable sadness.

Only later in the sunlight do we remember
  When a brook laughs with the same gentle eyes
  Or a frightened fawn leaps in sudden surprise
  Or a dog runs carelessly across a field,
  Remember
    An excited face and a loving heart,
    A death too soon and a life apart.
  Missing
    A presence and a touch
    And a smiling face so very much.
  Only grateful that he could stay as long
  Only grateful for the very special song
    He sang to us as long as he could live.
  Grateful above all
    That he walked easy on the earth.

The Lady Wins with Smiles

The lady wins with smiles and tears
   And seductive warmth,
Knowing all will be as she wants
   Until she doesn't want it.
If softness does not buy surrender,
   Sweetness swells to anger
   And a one-sided war.
As in puberty man is no match.
   He learned in the locker room
   That anger leads to blood and pain and murder.
Anger is on her side. All her teeth are intact.
   She does not fear the police
   Who are only more lusting men.
It is a destructive thing,
   This undeclared war between the sexes:
      Woman will hate the man she displaces,
      Man will hate himself crawling to her bed.
Who can teach us of love?
   Perhaps time and courage, and above all,
   An honest declaration of war.

I Wonder if Columbus

I wonder if Columbus would have discovered American in 1492
   If his wife hadn't nagged him
   To build a summer place in Naples.
Or if Shakespeare had such trouble ending *King Lear*
   Because he promised to help his brother-in-law
   Fix up his basement.
I wonder if Ben Franklin would have invented color television
   If the school hadn't kept calling
   About his son's antisocial behavior.
Or if Jesus couldn't heal a leper and two cripples
   Because his mother's parents
   Were coming for the Labor Day weekend.
I also wonder what the hell I'm doing
   Watching a Little League doubleheader
   Because my brother's kid might pinch-hit the second game.

Of Martyrs

Emma Burns is a martyr
   And stays with Jimmy
Only because she feels sorry for him, her folks like him,
   The neighbors expect it,
   And he takes their two boys fishing every Saturday.
Emma survives by a furtive affair with Frank Harris
   Every other Thursday afternoon.

Jimmy Burns is also a martyr
And stays with Emma
   Only because he feels sorry for her, his boss likes her,
   The neighbors expect it,
   And she is teaching the boys how to play the piano.
Jimmy survives by a furtive affair with Frank Harris's wife
   Every other Wednesday morning.

The Burns boys are also martyrs.
   They hate fishing,
     But feel sorry for their father.
   They also hate the piano,
     But don't want to hurt their mother's feelings.
They survive by smoking dope with the Harris kids.

Sin sure does have a way of keeping families together.

Musings on a Napkin in a Singles Bar

Lonely eyes lining up
  Taking
    What they can get,
Lonely lives signing up
  Clinging
    To what's left.
A hand to hold
  And silence filled with sound.
A secret told
  And a familiar smell around.
Maybe love tonight,
  An end
    To all the strain,
Maybe this one's right,
  And life
    Will start again.
So many faces look the same,
  So many conversations
    Heard before.
So many places without a name,
  So many hopes
    Left at the door.

The Mid-Life Crisis

According to psychological surveys, John is in a mid-life crisis.
He left Gert, his wife of twenty-six years, as a relic of a previous life,
And married a *Playboy* centerfold sans stretch marks or thigh bumps,
A beauty named Debbie—aren't they all—whose teeth shine
   like the flesh of a McIntosh apple,
Whose breasts are the two sipping fawns of Solomon's love poem,
And whose skin is so creamy John gives her welts with his
   drying forearms.
At first the mid-life crisis was only feeling silly in a custom
   tee-shirt with "Daddy digs Mama's pears" in four colors
And too tight jeans that made his testicles turn blue.
Later he aggravated an old hernia at an all-night disco,
Ruined Debbie's first vaginal orgasm with a burst of emphysema,
And scared hell out of her Doberman with a surgical skin stretching
   that forced him to bare permanently his newly capped teeth.
On a camping trip around the Mediterranean, he developed arthritis,
   pellagra, skin lice and was robbed in Turkey.
Although he attended rock and jazz concerts, EST, bought a wok,
   and learned to read tarot cards,

There was nothing to talk about and he sought psychic help
    When he compulsively had a Buddha tattooed around his navel.
After three visits to a holistic healer Debbie used to live with,
    the three of them began sleeping together in a giant waterbed,
Dined on rice and steamed vegetables, and traded mantras once a month.
When John did not improve, he called Gert and returned for a weekend.
After four martinis, pig hocks, sauerkraut, and a Dutch Master,
    John finally felt free enough to break air.
The stomach pains immediately subsided, he told Gert the whole story,
    and gave his Levis and beads to his teenaged son.
The next day he watched three football games with a six-pack,
    while Gert prepared his favorite foods and did the dishes.
He told her how great it was to be back, and slept soundly
    on an orthopedic mattress.
After a sausage omelette and four cups of coffee, John uncapped a beer
    and settled down to watch two more games.
Gert cleaned up the kitchen and kissed him softly on the forehead.
Then she gave him the house keys and went off to live with
    Debbie and the holistic healer.

The Typing Pool

The typing pool is peopled
   with hair spray and contact lenses
And joyful little ladies
   waiting for their princes.

   He will come, he will come,
   He will, he will,
   Riding a white stallion
   Up a long hill.

The typing pool is peopled
   with coffee breaks and cigarettes
And anxious little ladies
   falling deeper in debt.

   He will come, he will come,
   He will, he will,
   Riding a white stallion
   Up a long hill.

The typing pool is peopled
   with eye shadow and broken dreams
And silent little ladies
   typing over screams.

Suburban Sisters

Suburban sisters of the very clever sell,
Microwave ladies turned Southern belle,
   Sophisticated womanhood
   And sad as hell.

Tennis chatter and too much time,
Improving backhands and neglecting minds,
   I wonder what fossils
   The future will find.

Down with work and ERA,
Equal pay for equal play,
   Let's phone and ask Regina
   How to spend the day.

Bored sisters of the suburban scam,
Diet-rite cola and puppeteers of man,
   Not enough life
   For a decent epigram.

Suburban sisters of the very clever sell,
Microwave ladies turned Southern belle,
   Lonely, lost womanhood
   And sad as hell.

A Conversation

"Are you there, God?"
  She asked prayerfully.
"Sometimes,"
  He answered carefully.
"Do you care, God?"
  she asked faithfully.
"Not always,"
  He said playfully.
"But, you do believe, God?"
  she asked persistently.
"At times," He replied,
  "But not consistently."

Who Invented Love?

Who invented love
   And gave it a name beyond friendship?
Certainly not me,
   Distressed by too many words
   content to enjoy the birds
A good friend to have
   But loving so fearfully and badly.

Who invented love
   and gave it a passing grade beyond friendship?
Certainly not me,
   Finally out of school again
   Ignoring the golden rule again
A good friend to have
   But loving so fearfully and badly.

Love was someone's guile
   That pleased us for a while,
Then disappeared in sunsets without words.
   Or too many.

I like love without a name
   An unasked touch
   A childhood game
I like love that doesn't grade
   A sudden smile
   A new charade
I like love that never has to say
   "I love you."

"I need you moist and silent in my arms,
I need the cool sweetness of your face,
I need you before the noonday sun alarms,
   Or I will die in this desert of a place."

Since You've Gone

Since you've gone,
  Sadness descends like thick desert air
  In an unending heat wave of some immobility.
There is no refreshing breeze,
  Only the discordant screeching of a blackbird in the trees,
  His throat as dry as my heart,
  His rasping as monotonous as my thoughts.
Life is an effort now, each moment of silence a scream for you.
  Where did the mockingbird go?
  When will the sweet water flow in spring's raging rivulets?
Please come to me early in the morning,
  Come and share my bed without words or warning
  Before the sun rises to announce the day
  And the heat suffocates each fly and breath in its way.
A shade tree is not enough for me,
Not even cool water or a relieving breeze.
  I need you moist and silent in my arms,
  I need the cool sweetness of your face,
  I need you before the noonday sun alarms,
    Or I will die in this desert of a place.

Damn Those Old Movies

Damn those old movies that promised a happy ending,
   The sentimental and singing kind,
   The gentle, bells-are-ringing kind
That left me looking for a blue-eyed blonde in a bus station.

Damn those English novels that promised a perfect love,
   The sighing, silent, dramatic kind,
   The talking, totally franatic kind
That left me looking for Jane Eyre across a misty moor.

Damn that virgin Mary who promised an immaculate love,
   The reverent, sweetly maternal kind,
   The peaceful, softly eternal kind
That left me looking for a grinning madonna in the back pew.

Thus I was not prepared for Medea.
Or Delilah.
Or you.

Unisex

Unisex is out in force
  To dress the ladies like little boys,
  Hiding their breasts in Corduroy vests
  And squaring their shoulders.
  Derrieres are lost in tailored trousers,
  And even my favorite middle-aged male carousers
  Carry an extra hair dryer in the glove compartment
  And look almost too damn cute to drink with.
Miniskirts are but a memory.
  Gone the flash of hip, the tender thigh,
  The gasp at lunch, the bus stop sigh.
  I stand among equals, chauvinistically askance,
  Slapping on the back the ones I used to kiss,
  Searching for the innuendoes I sorely miss
  And wondering what happened to the pockets in my pants.

Alas! I will go away until the discos disappear,
Wait until the designers expose a rounded rear,
Search for a place where no one really cares
What unisex decides is the proper thing to wear.
I'll be gone until New York and Paris mend their ways,
  But I wonder what the closet queens are wearing these days?

California Girl

I've looked around a town or two
And I've wandered through the world,
   But I've never met the equal of
A California girl.
   She's open and still mysterious,
   Concerned but not too serious,
   She's class—without pretence
   And style—without offense,
Just a California girl.

She seems a little softer,
   Her laugh is more serene.
She talks a little slower
   And finds the time to dream.
She's a field beneath the freeways,
   A meadow in the maze,
A hill between the buildings,
   New York with country ways.
She can sit with me in silence,
   When there's nothing else to say.
She never talks of freedom,
   Because she lives it every day.

She's open and yet mysterious,
   Concerned but not too serious,
She's class—without pretence
   And style—without offense,
Just a California girl.

Last Chance at Love

So many loves
　　That never had a chance,
Too afraid to risk a little pain.
So many dreams
　　Were lost to circumstance,
Now they're gone and won't be back again.

　　Last chance at love, the eyes are moving on,
　　Soon there'll be just memories left to know.
　　Last chance at love, the skies are moving on,
　　And fantasy's a lonely way to go.

So many loves
　　That seemed to disappear,
It's hard to know which one could be the last.
So many dreams
　　Were lost in childish fear,
And now the future's shorter than the past.

　　Last chance at love, echoes fade away,
　　Soon there'll be just memories left to know.
　　Last chance at love, maybe it's today,
　　Fantasy's a lonely way to go.

Last chance
　　At love.

I Don't Know if I Love You

I don't know if I love you, but without you
   All my insecurities emerge like a sudden rash.
I'm not as handsome as I thought, nor as funny,
   Certainly not as brilliant in late-night opinions.
No one calls the lines in my face "nature's etchings"
   And I don't seem as gentle as before.
There's no one like you really to be angry at,
   And I can't seem to make anyone cry.
I didn't like my face this morning
   And my shoulders weren't as broad coming from the shower.

No one smiled at my new cowboy shirt and Cheyenne boots.
I seem shorter somehow, I noticed it in the bakery window.
And there's some fear in my eyes I'm afraid everyone will see.
Will you come back
   For a day
   Or a weekend
   Or forever
And tell me how beautiful I am?

"Walk easy on the earth:
  Love is waiting to reveal itself when it is time..."

Walk Easy on the Earth

Walk easy on the earth:
　　Each life has its own fragile rhythm,
　　To be aware of it is to understand,
　　To ignore it is to abandon oneself to sadness.
　　It is to search vainly for the wholeness
　　　　that only comes in surrender to what is.

Walk easy on the earth:
　　Too much seriousness obscures beauty,
　　Intensity blinds and distorts one's focus,
　　Excessive ambition destroys true perception.
　　It is not hard work or suffering that debilitates,
　　but a loss of contact with oneself.

Walk easy on the earth:
　　Anger clouds vision and rage shortens life,
　　Laughter is the greatest gift of the free spirit.
　　To laugh profoundly and often is to understand,
　　To laugh at oneself and all of life,
　　　　and thus to see clearly.

Walk easy on the earth:
　　Love is waiting to reveal itself when it is time,
　　Nor can one create it despite the most noble intent.
　　Love is the discovery of one's own rhythm in another.
　　Any other love, regardless of time or commitment,
　　　　will only be doomed and painful.

This above all: Walk easy on the earth!

Conclusion

Like most of you, I was born "walking" very easy on the earth. It took time and teaching to frighten me, and convert my joyful path into a narrow, painful one. With domestic turmoil and mounting fear came a need to *take control* of my life, lest I be lost in the chaos around me. To make sure I was loved and cared for, I began to deny and bury any feelings that were unacceptable to parents, teachers, and even peers. Only "nice" feelings were allowed.

And only when alone, or with my dog, did my real self emerge, then to be stuffed down my throat in various degrees when anyone else was around. I feared to admit that I was bored by daily Mass and hated the drudgery of football practice every fall. My studies gradually became far more discipline and competitive pressure than any love of learning, and even my dreams reflected others' expectations. And the most painful part was that I knew there was no one to tell.

Many years later have I learned that to *take control* is the opposite of *trust*. I had trusted no one, and with good reason. Every important person in my life handed me a blueprint which I must follow if I were to be loved. I had no real friends, because no one knew who I was. Even me. And under the usually unruffled and smiling surface was a very angry boy. Of course, even the rage had to be denied. I became the student and athlete, the priest and husband that tried to please everyone but myself.

What I became was a fraud, and probably would have remained so had not the pain been too much to endure, the anger too explosive to contain.

But even when I began to acknowledge who I was, help was not easy to find.

I looked everywhere but inside myself. I had to *turst!* But whom? I tried therapists and pills, books and exotic travels, success and nurturing women. All taught me something in bits and pieces, but there was still a heaviness I couldn't release.

Finally I've begun to trust the process of life, to know that a loving hand guides my steps, an inner voice speaks when I am silent enough to listen. I now know the guiding hand and inner voice are the God, by whatever name, I sought in years of prayerful pleading and an exhausting search. I've only had to let go of controls to become who I always was inside. Not in *doing* would I be healed, but in *undoing*. To walk easy is to flow with life, to stop pushing. To *trust*.

It has not been easy for me to bend with the river, but it hasn't been as hard as it was to pretend. If there were an easier way I would have taken it. I think I tried them all. And none do I regret, for the hand was there all the time. Shaping, calling, leading, and guiding me to the peace and joy of the person I really am. The journey is not over, but the voice still whispers, the hand is still outstretched. Now, at least, I've learned to *Walk Easy On The Earth*.

James Kavanaugh

INFORMATION ABOUT BOOKS AND TAPES AND APPEARANCES BY JAMES KAVANAUGH

The *Steven J. Nash Publishing Company* will supply you with all books and tapes of James Kavanaugh currently available. To receive information about James Kavanaugh's *new* books or tapes, lectures and workshops; to arrange appearances or TV and radio interviews; or for *The James Kavanaugh Newsletter*, write to:

STEVEN J. NASH PUBLISHING
P.O. Box 2115 • Highland Park, Illinois 60035
or Call: 1-800-843-8545

QUALITY PAPERBACK BOOKS OF JAMES KAVANAUGH
by STEVEN J. NASH:

There Are Men Too Gentle To Live Among Wolves *(65th Printing)* In this moving classic, Kavanaugh writes: "I am one of the searchers. There are, I believe, millions of us. We searchers are ambitious only for life itself, for everything beautiful it can provide...Most of all we want to love and to be loved, to live in a relationship that will not impede our wandering, nor prevent our search, nor lock us in prison walls..."

Will You Be My Friend? *(56th Printing)* Kavanaugh writes in this powerful, poetic reflection on true friendship: "Friendship is freedom, is flowing, is rare. It does not need stimulation, it stimulates itself. It trusts, understands, grows, explores, it smiles and weeps. It does not exhaust or cling, expect or demand. It is—and that is enough—and it dreams a lot!"

Laughing Down Lonely Canyons *(1986)* Kavanaugh brings his special blend of compassion, insight, and gentle humor to life's hard and hurting times...to those periods in our lives when we finally confront loneliness and fear... "This is a book for the barely brave like me, who refuse to abandon their dream...It is for those who want to make of life the joy it was meant to be, who refuse to give up no matter the pain..."

From Loneliness To Love *(1988)* At a time when the past freedoms grow dim, it seems hard to make intimate connections. There's a new kind of sexual warfare in which everyone loses the healing power of love. Kavanaugh writes: "To move from loneliness to love means to take a risk...to create the kind of personal environment and support we need. This is a book of hope and reassurance that love is available and loneliness can end."

Search: A Guide For Those Who Dare Ask of Life Everything Good and Beautiful. *(Prose, 1989)* "**Search** provides 12 proven principles to move from self doubt through self awareness to self love. It is a celebration of one's creativity and unique beauty, rising from practical psychology to the spiritual power of our Inner Being in a journey to wholeness." James Kavanaugh frequently offers an exciting workshop based on this book in various parts of the country.

Today I Wondered About Love *(formerly Will You Still Love Me)* This book was written in San Francisco and captured the soul of that city. Herein are some of Kavanaugh's most profound and gently humorous reflections on the man-woman experience. Burt Bacharach called this his "favorite Kavanaugh book."

Maybe If I Loved You More These passionate, lyrical poems confront forces that numb our senses and corrupt our values. Kavanaugh once again challenges us to be fully human, to move past private fears to simplicity and joy: "So much of life is spent trying to prove something...Maybe if I loved you more, I wouldn't have to prove anything!"

Sunshine Days and Foggy Nights This work contains Kavanaugh's most tender love poems, like the wondrous *Fragile Woman:* "too tender for sex, who will surely die—if tonight I do not love you." In words reminiscent of Joseph Campbell, he tells of the energy of any creative life: "The work I find most significant drains the least energy . . . my distractions are usually more creative than my resolutions."

Winter Has Lasted Too Long Kavanaugh sings of personal freedom and real love in a superb preface: "We shall be as free as we want, as mad as we are, as honest as we can. We shall accept no price for our integrity . . . This book is a heart's recognition that truth matters, love is attainable, and spring will begin tomorrow." Herein is the famed, "How much love I wasted on those I never loved."

Walk Easy On The Earth The book was inspired by three years Kavanaugh spent immersed in nature in a remote cabin in the California gold country. "I do not focus on the world's despair," he writes. "I am forever renewed by spring splashing over granite rocks, or a cautious deer emerging into twilight. I know then that I will survive all my personal fears and realize my finest dreams."

A Village Called Harmony—A Fable A powerful, eloquent prose tale that touches the deepest chords in the human struggle of lust and love, passion and peace. Dear Abby says: "It is a powerful tale of our times. A classic! I loved it!" The Detroit Free Press says: "Kavanaugh spins a sentence until it sings."

Celebrate the Sun: A Love Story A moving prose allegory about the life of Harry Langendorf Pelican, dedicated to "those who take time to celebrate the sun—and are grateful!" Alan Watts called it: "A stirring and unforgettable story that unites wondrously the wisdom of East and West."

The Crooked Angel James Kavanaugh's only children's story, newly illustrated in four colors, tells of two angels "with crooked little wings" who escape from isolation and sadness through friendship and laughter. A particular Christmas delight that sold out wherever it was displayed. Says Goldie Hawn: "My children loved it! So did I."

The Tears and Laughter Of A Man's Soul *(1990 Hardback)* "His most mature and personal ever!"—LA TIMES. With the power that has won "thousands of readers who never liked poetry before."—SAN FRAN. CHRONICLE. Kavanaugh touches our hearts, gently leading us from anxiety and near despair to love, laughter, courage and hope. He reveals a faith beyond dogmas, leading to the profound experience of "the Power within." He makes us laugh aloud and weeps with us in our struggle for freedom and peace. He writes as a man "whose theories have been tested in the laboratory of vast experience"—TAMPA TRIBUNE. The man who 20 years ago challenged religions and culture itself, emerges as a brave explorer whose struggles reflect the joy and hope of the human spirit. This is no book of poetic rhetoric, but "a saga of life and near death, scars and victory, falling and forever rising! It is the *tears and laughter of a man's soul!*"